My
Mawlid

an Early Reader for Muslim Children
& Mawlid Play for Children

Elizabeth Bootman

DEDICATION
for my little dragons

Muslim Early Readers are designed to fit the unique context of young Muslims learning to read with short, simple words and sentences. For more ideas on how to teach young Muslims please see our website.

https://sirajunmunira.wordpress.com

I learn the sira for

Mawlid.

I light lanterns for

Mawlid.

I bake a cake for

Mawlid.

The angels bring
gifts for Mawlid.

I make a banner for

Mawlid.

I hang lights for

Mawlid.

I sing songs for

Mawlid.

The Prophet (s) was born in the year of the elephant.

The birds came to

fan Amina (r).

The cloud came to carry the Prophet (s) around the world.

The fish Zalmusa

danced in the Sea.

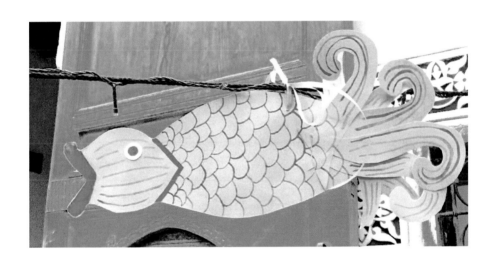

Mawlid Play for Children Script in English and French:

Mawlid Adaptation for The Light of Muhammad by Hajjah Amina Adil.

In the year of the elephant the Prophet (s) was born.

– wave the elephant puppet

A king named Abraha brought an army to destroy the Kaba. Mahmud the elephant refused to destroy the Kaba and sat down on the ground.

– wave the elephant puppet

The time for the Prophet (s) to be born was near and many holy ladies came to help Amina (r) the mother of the Prophet (s).

A flock of birds came to fan her with their wings and flew around her in circles.

– wave the bird puppets

The Prophet (s) was born and he immediately prayed for us.

A white cloud came that sounded like galloping horses and took the prophet around the world and then brought him back to his mother Amina (r).

– wave the cloud puppets

An angel came and whispered secrets in the Prophet's (s) ear.

The fish named Zalmusa, with 70 thousand

heads and 70 thousand tails, danced in the sea with joy that the Prophet (s) had arrived.

– wave the fish puppet
A king and his daughter came to see the newborn baby in Mecca.

The whole world celebrated the birth of the Prophet (s).
And now we will celebrate the birth of the Prophet (s) with sweets and gifts and salawat!

(This would be a very good time to have a song.)

Extrait du livre Light of Muhammad (Hajjah Amina Adil). Adaptation pour le Mawlid.

Durant l'année de l'éléphant, le Prophète (s) est né.

– Agitez les marionnettes d'éléphants

Un roi qui s'appelait Abraha regroupa une armée pour détruire la Kaba.

Mahmud l'éléphant refusa de détruire la Kaba et il décida de s'assoir parterre.

– Agitez les marionnettes d'éléphants

La naissance du Prophète (s) s'approchait et beaucoup de femmes saintes sont venues aider Amina (r) la mère du Prophète (s).

Un groupe d'oiseaux sont venus la rafraîchir en agitant leurs ailes et ont volé autour d'elle en faisant des cercles.

– Agitez les marionnettes d'oiseaux

Le Prophète (s) est né et il a tout de suite prié pour nous.
Un nuage blanc qui faisait le bruit de chevaux qui galopent est venu. Il a emmené le Prophète (s) autour du monde et l'a ramené à sa mère Amina (r).

– Agitez les marionnettes du nuage

Un ange est venu et a chuchoté des secrets dans l'oreille du Prophète (s).

Un poisson qui s'appelait Zalmusa, qui avait 70 mille têtes et 70 mille queues, a dansé dans la mer tellement il était heureux que le Prophète (s) soit arrivé.

– Agitez les marionnettes du poisson

Un roi et sa fille sont venus voir le nouveau-né à la Mecque.

Le monde entier a célébré la naissance du Prophète (s).
Et aujourd'hui nous allons célébrer la naissance du Prophète (s) avec des bonbons, des cadeaux et des salawats! Alors chantons une salawat pour notre Prophète (s)!

(Un bon moment pour chanter une chanson, ex : Tala al Badru Alayna….)

Please see our plays, projects
and books at

sirajunmunira.wordpress.com

My Turban: An Early Reader for Muslim Children

ISBN-13: 978-1549928000, **ISBN-10:** 1549928007

 (1)

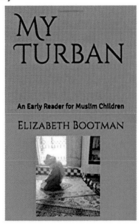

The Pool of Paradise: A 30 Day Curriculum

ISBN-13: 978-1549951756, **ISBN-10:** 1549951750

⭐⭐⭐⭐⭐ (1)

DERVISH
DOLLS
SIRAJUNMUNIRA.WORDPRESS.COM

THE TREE
OF
PROPHETS

Made in United States
North Haven, CT
10 October 2022

25250729R00024